A Bark In The Park

A Guide For Walking Your Dog In Delaware County

DOUG GELBERT

illustrations by
ANDREW CHESWORTH

CRUDEN BAY

About This Guide:

Have you ever considered how far you walk in a lifetime with your dog? If you walk just 20 minutes a day, in ten years you will have walked far enough to cover the United States coast to coast. With all that walking you are going to be on the lookout for variety.

This guide highlights 30 parks I refer to as "destination parks." These are not the local neighborhood parks where you go for your daily walk. I have selected 22 parks with trails within Delaware County and another eight in neighboring counties within a 30-minute drive of county borders.

Each park is rated on its desirability for dog-walking on a scale of one to four "hikers." These are my personal ratings and reflect my bias solely (Katie, my Border Collie/German Shepherd mix, would give them all four hikers). Roughly, they mean:

ONE HIKER	Not worth driving to.
TWO HIKERS	Worth stopping at if you're nearby.
THREE HIKERS	Worth driving to.
FOUR HIKERS	Worth planning a special dog/owner outing.

And, truth be told, any new trail is more exciting than even the most pleasant of familiar walks. So grab that leash and start walking!
DBG

• •

A BARK IN THE PARK

Copyright 2000 by Cruden Bay Books

All rights reserved. No part of this book may be reproduced or transmitted in any form or by any means, electronic or mechanical, including photocopying, recording or by any information storage and retrieval system without permission in writing from the Publisher.

Cruden Bay Books
PO Box 467
Montchanin, DE 19710

International Standard Book Number 0-9644427-1-X

Manufactured in the United States of America

Inside:

Delaware County Parks

Brooke Farm Trail	4
Clayton Park	6
Darlington Trail	8
Glen Providence Park	10
Governor Printz Park	12
Hildacy Farm	14
Indian Orchard & Linvill Trails	16
John Heinz National Wildlife Refuge	18
Main Line Colleges	20
Morton Homestead	22
Newlin Grist Mill	24
Ridley Creek State Park	26
Rose Tree Park	28
Scott Arboretum	30
Skunk Hollow Trails	32
Smedley Park	34
Springfield Trail	36
Taylor Arboretum	38
Tyler Arboretum	40
Upland Park	42
Wawa Preserve	44
Woodlawn Trustees Property	46

Parks Nearby

Andorra Nature Center/Fairmount Park	48
Brandywine Creek State Park	50
Fair Hill Natural Resources Management Area	52
French Creek State Park	54
Oakburne Park	56
Riverbend Environmental Education Center	58
Valley Forge National Historic Park	60
White Clay Creek State Preseve/State Park	62

Delaware County Parks

BROOKE FARM TRAIL

THE PARK:
Radnor Township created this trail in woodlands squeezed by residential development.

WALKS:
This is a linear trail that explores the bottomlands around the Little Darby Creek.

TRAIL TIME?
Less than an hour.

TRAIL TERRAIN?
After a quick descent from the trailhead this is flat walking throughout.

TRAIL SURFACE?
Dirt.

TRAIL SENSE?
The trail is well-blazed and the trailhead is marked by a universal hiking sign.

SWIMMING?
The Little Darby is a pleasant waterway but not deep enough for more than splashing.

ADMISSION FEE:
None.

> **BONUS**
> A shy, nervous creature, the red fox is not often seen on the trails, especially with a dog along, but one lives in these hemmed-in woods. In good times, the fox will nosh on mice and squirrels and rabbits but will also be satisfied with such humble fare as insects and berries. Look for him anytime during the day but especially during the evening.

PARK HOURS:
Dawn to dusk.

DIRECTIONS:
Brooke Farm Trail is in western Radnor Township. The trailhead is at the interesection of Wayne Avenue and Maplewood Road. Parking is available in the front parking lot of the Wayne Elementary School opposite the trailhead.

Best Parks To Take The Dog Swimming

1. Morton Homestead
2. John Heinz National Wildlife Refuge
3. Woodlawn Trustees Property
4. Ridley Creek State Park
5. Governor Printz Park

CLAYTON PARK

THE PARK:
Clayton Park began life in 1957 as a 59-acre gift from Mrs. Nelson Clayton. Today, at 170 acres, it is the largest of Delaware County's parks, with most of the acreage given to recreational pursuits such as golf and softball.

WALKS:
A short multi-use trail loops through the trees around the parking lot. It is shaded and pleasant and good for walking the dog and pushing the baby stroller. A narrow, somewhat scruffy nature trail winds through the beech/maple climax forest. You can also bushwhack to the far regions of the Featherbed Lane area of the park.

TRAIL TIME?
Less than an hour.

> **BONUS**
> The trail passes hard by the 7th hole of the golf course where you can watch players pit their talent against a tricky, mid-length par-3. Dogs and golf courses have a long history dating to the Scottish sheep-herding origins of the game. While dogs are not welcome on American courses, it is still rare to find a local links in Scotland without a resident, golf-savvy dog.

TRAIL TERRAIN?
Most of the hills at Clayton Park are out on the golf course; the trails are easy walking.

TRAIL SURFACE?
The multi-use trail is paved; the trails through the woods are dirt and grass.

TRAIL SENSE?
The trails are not marked but seldom do you walk out of sight of the parking lot.

SWIMMING?
A small branch of the Green Creek runs along the multi-use trail. It is not deep enough for swimming but is good for jumping in and cooling off.

ADMISSION FEE:
None.

PARK HOURS:
8:00 a.m. - sunset, year-round.

DIRECTIONS:
Clayton Park is in Concord Township on Route 322 (Conchester Highway) between I-95 and Route 1. To reach the parking lot, take Garnet Mine Road off Route 322 and continue for 1/2 mile to the entrance on the right.

DARLINGTON TRAIL

THE PARK:
The Darlington Trail, developed by Middletown Township, rims the former Darlington Family Dairy Farm.

WALKS:
Half of the yellow-blazed Darlington Trail hugs the heavily wooded Chester Creek valley and other half traverses the meadows and fields of the former farmstead. The entire loop is approximately 2 3/4 miles long. The Cornucopia Trail, a shorter path blazed in orange, connects with the Darlington Trail and circumnavigates a residential area. The Darlington Trail also connects with the Rocky Run Trail, running east to the Tyler Arboretum. The trails, for the most part, are wide and easy to negotiate.

TRAIL TIME?
More than one hour.

TRAIL TERRAIN?
To do the entire loop will require several steep climbs away from Chester Creek. You can also treat the trail as a linear hike along the creekbed which creates an easy walk.

TRAIL SURFACE?
Dirt and grass; some rocky stretches.

TRAIL SENSE?
The trails are well-marked; there is a detailed map posted on the board at the trailhead.

SWIMMING?
The Chester Creek is extremely scenic through the property and at times is wide enough and deep enough for an extended doggie dip. Rocky Run, which joins the Chester Creek on the trail is more for splashing.

> **BONUS**
> At a 270-degree turn in the Chester Creek behind the parking lot, the banks are wide and sandy, giving your dog the opportunity for a rare Delaware County beach experience.

ADMISSION FEE:
　None.

PARK HOURS:
　Sunrise - sunset, year-round.

DIRECTIONS:
　Darlington Trail is in Middletown Township. A small parking lot for the Darlington Trail is located on Darlington Road, 1/2 mile from Route 1. The parking lot is well-marked by a trailhead sign.

How To Pet A Dog

Tickling tummies slowly and gently works wonders. Never use a rubbing motion; this makes dogs bad-tempered. A gentle tickle with the tips of the fingers is all that is necessary to induce calm in a dog. I hate strangers who go up to dogs with their hands held to the dog's nose, usually palm towards themselves. How does the dog know that the hand doesn't hold something horrid? The palm should always be shown to the dog and go straight down to between the dog's front legs and tickle gently with a soothing voice to acompany the action. Very often the dog raises its back leg in a scratching movement, it gets so much pleasure from this.

*　　　　　　　　　　　　　　　　-Barbara Woodhouse*

GLEN PROVIDENCE PARK

THE PARK:
This historic park was Delaware County's first, established in 1935 as the result of a gift of 30 acres from George Butler. Butler was a later owner of the Broomall House, the 1873 Victorian home of the former United States Congressman and friend of Abraham Lincoln, John Broomall.

WALKS:
There are a series of short, linear trails in this wooded enclave. The trails do not loop and dead-end at park boundaries.

TRAIL TIME?
Less than an hour.

TRAIL TERRAIN?
A steep slope leads down away from the parking lot but the trails are fairly easy walking.

TRAIL SURFACE?
Dirt.

TRAIL SENSE?
The trails are not marked and no trail map is available. The trails all dead-end against the roads surrounding the park.

SWIMMING?
A shallow creek wanders through the property from Broomall Lake to Ridley Creek but it is not suitable for swimming.

Dogs' lives are too short. Their only fault, really.
-Agnes Sligh Turnbull

> **BONUS**
> The dual entrance stairways to Glen Providence Park create an elegant entree to strolling this public space.

ADMISSION FEE:
　　None.

PARK HOURS:
　　8:00 a.m.-sunset, year round.

DIRECTIONS:
　　Glen Providence Park is in the western end of Media, at the end of State Street, 1 1/2 blocks off Baltimore Pike. There is street parking in front of the park.

GOVERNOR PRINTZ PARK

THE PARK:
In the 1630s Sweden was a great European power but was lagging behind in the race to colonize the new world. King Gustavus Adolphus laid plans for a "New Sweden" but was killed in battle in 1632. It took another five years before the *Kalmar Nyckel* and the *Vogel Grip* set sail for America. The Swedes settled in Wilmington and in 1643 a new governor named Johan Printz arrived to command the colony. Immediately, Printz, a strong and energetic leader, expanded New Sweden and founded the first permanent settlement in Pennsylvania here.

WALKS:
This small park is included because it offers the only access to swimming in the Delaware River in Delaware County. Steps lead to the river, still subject to tidal action here, and a small, muddy beach. There is a short history path with exhibits on the settling of Pennsylvania.

TRAIL TIME?
Less than an hour.

TRAIL TERRAIN?
Flat.

> **BONUS**
> Johan Printz made his headquarters at New Sweden near this park. It was once thought that his large two-story home, Printzhof, was located here but no evidence of the building has ever been uncovered. The "Path to Printzhof" turns the struggles and triumphs of Pennsylvania's first colony into a life-size board game using coin flips. Your well-trained dog can even play as well.

TRAIL SURFACE?
   Grass.

TRAIL SENSE?
   None needed.

SWIMMING?
   The Delaware River is better suited to boating than swimming at this point but it is deep enough for a good doggie aquatic workout.

ADMISSION FEE:
   None.

PARK HOURS:
   8:00 a.m. - sunset, year-round.

DIRECTIONS:
   Governor Printz Park is in Essington. Take Exit 9 off of I-95 and Route 420 South (Wanamaker Avenue). Continue to the end on 2nd Street, make a right and the park is two blocks on the left.

My dog can bark like a Congressman, fetch like an aide, beg like a press secretary and play dead like a receptionist.
                                                        -Gerald Solomon

HILDACY FARM

THE PARK:
>The Hildacy Farm, which dates from the early 19th century, was donated by Cyril and Hilda Fox to the Natural Lands Trust, which uses the buildings as its headquarters. The total acreage is 55.

WALKS:
>About two miles of trails traverse the meadows, horse pastures and shaded streams of Hildacy Farm. This is the best open-field hiking in Delaware County.

TRAIL TIME?
>Less than one hour.

TRAIL TERRAIN?
>There are some moderate hills on the gently sloping property.

TRAIL SURFACE?
>Mostly grass.

TRAIL SENSE?
>The trails are not marked but there is little chance of needing 911; a trail map is available.

SWIMMING?
>The millpond is for looking but there is access to the Crum Creek in the corner of the property.

ADMISSION FEE:
>None.

PARK HOURS/PHONE:
>Dawn to dusk. (610.353.5587)

BONUS
The fastest growing hardwood tree in the world is the paulownia, where it is said in its native China, "It looks like a pole in one year, an umbrella in three and can be sawn into boards in five years." Pennsylvania is at the northern reaches of its successful range and there is a paulownia plantation at Hildacy featuring the trees with enormous leaves and honey-producing flowers.

DIRECTIONS:
Hildacy Farm is in Newtown Township. From Route 1 go north on Route 252. Cross the dam at Springton Reservoir and immediately turn right onto Palmers Road. Enter the preserve via the first driveway on the right.

INDIAN ORCHARD & LINVILL TRAILS

THE PARK:
In 1986, Middletown Township began preserving significant portions of open space in Middletown in recognition of the Township's Tricentennial. These trails were carved from 157 acres of property acquired from the Linvill family.

WALKS:
The Indian Orchard Trail, blazed in yellow, loops through a woodlands of mature hardwoods and conifers, crossing five bridges along its one-mile length. The Linvill Trail covers 3 1/2 miles over two sections; one, a long perimeter loop around the pasturelands and orchards, the other a fish-hook trail behind Linvilla Orchard. A short spur connects the two trails.

TRAIL TIME?
More than an hour for the Linvill Trail; less than an hour to loop Indian Orchard.

TRAIL TERRAIN?
These trails are easy hiking, with the Linvill Trail the flatter of the two. Indian Orchard features some sporty ups and downs.

TRAIL SURFACE?
Mostly dirt and grass; beware on the Farm Fields Trail which is sometimes cut from the crop stalks, leaving tiny spears that can injure a pet's paws.

TRAIL SENSE?
The trails are marked but not always distinct when the blazes are on young trees in regenerating woods. The best trail map in Delaware County is available from the township office.

> **BONUS**
> Even into the 20th century indoor plumbing was not universal and the "necessary" or "outhouse" was a familiar sight on the rural American landscape. In the woods along the Indian Orchard Trail is a relic of these times - an abandoned two-seater necessary.

SWIMMING?
Crum Run intercepts the Indian Orchard Trail several times although it is not deep enough for a full swim. The most water you'll encounter on the Linville Trail is at the Hidden Hollow Swim Club, which doesn't welcome dogs in its pools.

ADMISSION FEE:
None.

PARK HOURS:
Sunrise - sunset, year-round.

DIRECTIONS:
The trails are south of Lima, just off Route 352 (Middletown Road). The parking lot for the Indian Orchard Trail is at the end of Copes Lane on the western side of Route 352. To reach the Linville Trail from Route 1, make a right on West Knowlton Road and take your first right on Linville Road to the parking lot.

JOHN HEINZ NATIONAL WILDLIFE REFUGE AT TINICUM

THE PARK:
There are more than 500 National Wildlife Refuges in the United States and only Philadelphia and San Francisco offer an urban environmental study. When the Swedes settled here in 1634, Tinicum Marsh measured over 5,700 acres. Three hundred years later the tidal marsh had been reduced to only 200 acres. The routing of I-95 in 1969 threatened to finish off the marsh but, in ironic fact, saved it. Congress authorized the purchase of 1,200 acres in 1972, establishing the Tinicum National Environmental Center and enabling the highway to roar through the area.

WALKS:
You can cover about ten miles of trails here in two major loops. The more attractive of the two is around the Impoundment marsh near the Visitor Contact Station. If you have a patient dog you can pause at the Observation Platform or one of the Observation Blinds and try to identify one of the 288 species of birds seen in the refuge.

The western loop, which begins in Delaware County, leads onto a dike in the middle of the marsh and along the Darby Creek. The trail on the dike is narrow to the point of being overgrown during the spring and summer.

TRAIL TIME?
More than an hour.

TRAIL TERRAIN?
Flat everywhere.

TRAIL SURFACE?
Dirt and grass, with long stretches of gravel road.

> **BONUS**
> There aren't many other places where you can walk along and scan the skies alternately for a Northern Goshawk and a McDonnell-Douglas or a Buff-Breasted Sandpiper and a Boeing.

TRAIL S:
The trail is not marked nor blazed but there is a map available. It is not detailed and expect to take a detour or two near the Route 420 parking area. Also, when walking along I-95, keep to the highway side of the chain link fence.

SWIMMING?
The Darby Creek is accessible but the fish pulled from these waters are contaminated so you may want to limit water time here.

ADMISSION FEE:
None.

PARK HOURS/PHONE:
8:00 a.m. - sunset, year-round. (215.365.3118)

DIRECTIONS:
Take I-95 North. Take Exit 10, Route 291 (Philadelphia International Airport). At the first light make a left onto Bartram Avenue. At the third light make a left onto 84th Street. At the second light make a left onto Lindbergh Boulevard. Make a right into the refuge just past the stop sign. The parking area in Delaware County is on Route 420; take Exit 9B off I-95 for Route 420 North. The parking area is right there.

MAIN LINE COLLEGES

THE PARK:
>When school is not in session, there are few better walks than around a deserted college campus. Several private colleges along the Main Line welcome responsible dog owners to visit campus.

WALKS:
>*Bryn Mawr College Arboretum.* This English-landscape-style campus mixes massive trees with its Gothic buildings. The campus grounds were designed by the firm of Frederick Law Olmstead, architects of many of America's greatest parks.

>*Haverford College Arboretum.* Once the center of the Welsh Tract, a prominent group of Quakers purchased 198.5 acres here in 1831. Two years later Haverford College was founded, making it the oldest institution of higher learning with Quaker roots in the country. There are two walking choices here: a nearly three-mile loop around the perimeter of the campus (you'll barely see any buildings) or an Arboretum tour highlighting 33 special trees.

>*Rosemont College.* At 56 acres, the smallest of the Main Line grounds, Rosemont offers a quiet walk around the knob of a hill. At the center of campus is Rathalla, resplendent with its French Renaissance turrets. The original house on the Sinnott Estate, it once contained all college activities.

>*Villanova Arboretum.* The oldest and largest Catholic university in Pennsylvania formally dedicated its arboretum in 1993 - more than 100 years after many of the school's 1,500 trees were well-established. The trees are easily identified from the paths.

TRAIL TIME?
>Less than an hour; although you can spend more than an hour at Haverford on the Nature Trail.

> **BONUS**
> These four colleges are close enough to one another that they all may be enjoyed in an afternoon.

TRAIL TERRAIN?
  It is easy walking through all the colleges.

TRAIL SURFACE?
  Most of the time is spent on paved walkways although the Nature Trail at Haverford is dirt.

TRAIL SENSE?
  Bryn Mawr, Haverford and Villanova have numerous map boards. The only formal trail is at Haverford and is actually 3/4 of a loop which must be completed by ducking through some back parking lots; a campus map and brochure are available.

SWIMMING?
  There are small streams at Haverford and Rosemont but no canine swimming on campus.

ADMISSION FEE:
  None.

PARK HOURS:
  Dawn to Dusk.

DIRECTIONS:
  From East to West: Haverford is on Route 30. Follow the signs to the Visitor Parking Lot where you can pick up a campus map and the trailhead. Bryn Mawr is three blocks north of Route 30 via Roberts Road. Parking is on the street. Rosemont College is on Montgomery Avenue; visitor parking is to the left of the entrance. Villanova is spread across Routes 30 and 320. The main parking lot is opposite the campus on Route 30.

MORTON HOMESTEAD

THE PARK:
This area was first cleared for settlement in the winter of 1654-1655 under the direction of Johan Rising, Governor of the colony of New Sweden. Morton Mortensson built a cabin on this site around 1672.

The historical significance of the Morton Homestead was first brought to public attention as early as 1862 when it was thought that John Morton, a signer of the Declaration of Independence, was born here. A century passed and in 1957 historians reluctantly concluded that there was no evidence of Morton's birth at this location on the banks of the Darby Creek. Undaunted, local boosters touted the structure as a fine example of a Swedish colonial log house. Alas, researchers in 1988 put the kibosh on that claim as well. Today, the Morton Homestead stands as one of the first truly American buildings - a melting pot of European influences.

WALKS:
The walk here doesn't even take five minutes - it is just a short loop around the cabin - but the Morton Homestead is included for its excellent access to a wide Darby Creek, providing as close to a canine lake swimming experience as there is in Delaware County.

TRAIL TIME?
Less than an hour.

TRAIL TERRAIN?
A flat little walk.

TRAIL SURFACE?
Paved stone and boardwalk.

TRAIL SENSE?
You can see the entire trail when you step out of your car.

BONUS
In some cases archeologists dig up answers to some question and in others they merely unearth more questions. While digging in 1988, scientists discovered the nearly intact "corduroy' log landing area most likely used by Jonas Morton in operating his ferry across Darby Creek. They also found a 14'8" by 10'4" rectangular hole cut into the bedrock. What was this hard-earned room used for? Special storage? A sauna? One clue comes from a legal correspondence dated April 3, 1678: "Jan Cornelissen of Amosland complayning to ye court that his son Erik is bereft of his natural senses and is turned quyt madd and yt hee being a poor man is not able to maintain him...ordered that three or four persons bee hired to build a little blockhouse at Amosland for to put in said madman." Was the Morton Homestead hole the cell used to hold Mad Erik?

SWIMMING?
If not the most scenic, the Darby Creek at the Morton Homestead is the widest and deepest canine swimming hole in Delaware County.

ADMISSION FEE:
None.

PARK HOURS/PHONE:
8:00 a.m. - sunset, year-round. (610.583.7221)

DIRECTIONS:
Morton Homestead is in Prospect Park. The park is on Route 420 (Wanamaker Avenue), just north of I-95, Exit 9.

A door is what a dog is perpetually on the wrong side of.
-James Thurber

NEWLIN MILL PARK

THE PARK:
   In 1704, Nathaniel Newlin built a stone grist mill and dam on the headwaters of the West Branch of Chester Creek. The modest mill continued to ground flour commercially until 1941. In 1957, E. Mortimer Newlin, 9th in descent from the Newlin patriarch, Nicholas, who was granted 500 acres of land here in 1685, bought the mill. He created the Nicholas Newlin Foundation to preserve this cornerstone of American colonial life. Today the park encompasses 150 acres.

WALKS:
   The trail leads through the grounds of the restored mill along the mill race. Once across the dam, the trails, about three miles in total, branch out through woods and fields, including the Christmas tree nursery.

TRAIL TIME?
   Less than an hour.

TRAIL TERRAIN?
   The trail by the waterside is flat and climbs to the back of the property on the opposite side of the mill race.

TRAIL SURFACE?
   Dirt and grass.

TRAIL SENSE?
   None of the trails is marked and there is no trail map. A map of the property is available, however, to help you navigate your way.

SWIMMING?
   There is doggie dipping available in Chester Creek, especially behind the dam.

> **BONUS**
> A regular planting of unusual trees, shrubs and wildflowers is executed each year at Newlin Mill. Today you can see a grove of California redwoods and sequoias and representatives of the three true cedars in the world: *Cedurs atlantica, C. deodora* and *C. libanotica*. The native trees are impressive as well - they include a giant ash and giant oak that were here before Nicholas Newlin emigrated from Ireland in 1683.

ADMISSION FEE:
   None for the trails.

PARK HOURS/PHONE:
   8:00 a.m. - sunset, year-round. (610.459.2359)

DIRECTIONS:
   Newlin Mill Park is seven miles southwest of Media, on Route 1 at the intersection with South Cheyney Road.

Best Parks To Hike More Than An Hour With The Dog

1. Tyler Arboretum
2. Woodlawn Trustees Property
3. Ridley Creek State Park
4. Darlington Trail
5. John Heinz National Wildlife Refuge

RIDLEY CREEK STATE PARK

THE PARK:
Settlement in this area dates back to the 1600s when villages grew around the mills sprinkled along the creeks and streams. Much of the park's 2,606 acres were consolidated in the Jefford's family - their "Hunting Hill" mansion, built in 1914 around a 1789 stone farmhouse, now serves as the park office. The commonwealth of Pennsylvania purchased the property in the 1960s - including 35 historic residences - and the park was dedicated in 1972.

WALKS:
Ridley Creek features 12 miles of hiking on four main trails. The White Trail visits most of the areas of the park and the others intersect this loop trail at many points. At its southern end the Yellow Trail connects with the trails of the adjacent Tyler Arboretum. A 5-mile multi-use loop is shared with bicyclists and joggers. Also, an unmarked trailhead just east of Ridley Creek on Gradyville Road offers one of the longest creekside walks in the area. CAUTION: These heavily wooded trails are narrow in many places and you and the dog will be prime targets for hitchhiking ticks.

TRAIL TIME?
More than an hour.

TRAIL TERRAIN?
Most of the trails wind through rolling woodland and meadows. You'll be moving up and down often but only an occasional hardy climb is necessary.

TRAIL SURFACE?
Mostly dirt; the multi-use trail is paved.

TRAIL SENSE?
The trails are blazed and easy to follow, except through the parking areas - keep your eye on the pavement here. A trail map is available.

> **BONUS**
> Along the multi-use trail are metal doggie
> water bowls chained to the benches.

SWIMMING?
Ridley Creek, while extremely scenic, is a relatively minor feature of hiking at Ridley Creek State Park. It is deep enough for swimming when the trail touches upon it. There are no ponds on the property.

ADMISSION FEE:
None.

PARK HOURS/PHONE:
8 a.m. - sunset, year-round. (610.892.3900)

DIRECTIONS:
The park can be accessed from Route 3, 2.5 miles west of Newtown Square, past the Colonial Pennsylvania Plantation. The park may also be entered from Gradyville Road - east from Route 352 or west from Route 252.

ROSE TREE PARK

THE PARK:
The Rose Tree Hunt Club, the oldest continuous fox-hunt club in America, was first organized here in 1859 by a group who met at the Rose Tree Tavern. The Club bought the inn, which maintained its own pack of hounds, in 1873. There was a trotting track on the grounds in the 1860s and in 1926 a new clubhouse and steeplechase track were added.

By the 1960s, more and more houses were rapidly cutting down the Club's hunting range. On April 9, 1964 the Rose Tree Hunt Club staged its last meet here before moving to York County. Delaware County subsequently purchased the land from Charles Leedon for a 120-acre park. Once a year the Rose Tree Hunt Club returns with its hounds and horses for a ceremonial meet.

WALKS:
The informal trails cross fields leading to a small wooded area in the middle of the park. This is more a park for romping with the dog than hiking.

TRAIL TIME?
Less than an hour.

TRAIL TERRAIN?
There are few flat stretches at Rose Tree Park but the hills are wide and rolling.

TRAIL SURFACE?
Grass across the hills and dirt through the woods.

TRAIL SENSE?
None of the trails is marked; the park is more for rambling than channeling down predetermined routes.

BONUS

No thoroughbred race horse ever captured the American imagination like Man o'War. When he died in 1947 at the age of 30, the large chestnut colt was embalmed and lay in state for two days. As many as 2,000 people attended his funeral and the burial service was broadcast nationally. Man o'War raced for only two years - in 1919 and 1920 - and so completely crushed the opposition that in five races only one other horse dared enter. He beat one of those cheeky rivals by an estimated 100 lengths. His only loss in 21 races was to a colt named Upset and afterwards, whenever an unexpected team won a sports event, it was an "upset." His owner, Samuel Riddle, who purchased Man o'War for $5,000 as a yearling at the urging of his wife, brought the great horse to Rose Tree Hunt Club in October 1920 before retiring him to stud. Some 30,000 people, including Bill Tilden and Jack Dempsey, turned out to see Man o'War here.

SWIMMING?
   The small stream, a branch of the Crum Creek, slices a valley through the wooded area but is not deep enough for a canine dip.

ADMISSION FEE:
   None.

PARK HOURS:
   Sunrise - sunset, year-round.

DIRECTIONS:
   Rose Tree Park is in Upper Providence Township. From Route 1 (Media Bypass), take Route 252 (Providence Road) to the park entrances on the right, just past Rose Tree Road.

SCOTT ARBORETUM

THE PARK:
The 300-acre Swarthmore campus is developed to be an arboretum, established in 1929 as a living memorial to Arthur Hoyt Scott, Class of 1895. The 3,000 different kinds of plants have been chosen as suggestions for the best trees, shrubs, perennials and annuals to use in home gardens in the Delaware Valley.

WALKS:
Several area colleges welcome responsible dog owners - Swarthmore's Scott Arboretum is the best walk. The collections are integrated with the stone buildings of the college which dates to 1864. There are also trails through the 200-acre Crum Woods, where your dog need only be under voice control. You'll find dog water bowls at the drinking fountains here, too.

TRAIL TIME?
More than an hour.

TRAIL TERRAIN?
The walk around campus is level; Crum Woods is situated on a steep hillside, but the trails leading to the water are well-graded.

TRAIL SURFACE?
All the surfaces on campus are paved. The trails in Crum Woods are mostly dirt but can also be broken macadam and stone.

TRAIL SENSE?
There are no trail markings but a detailed campus map is available.

SWIMMING?
Crum Creek is deep enough to permit canine swimming.

ADMISSION FEE:
None.

BONUS
In the far southwestern area of campus, beyond the holly collection, is a meadow containing a Swarthmore version of Stonehenge. Like the original, its origins are mysterious. From the slate bench you can chance to see the SEPTA trolley rolling across a 50-foot trestle over Crum Creek.

ADMISSION FEE:
   None.

PARK HOURS/PHONE:
   Dawn to dusk, year-round. (610.328.8025)

DIRECTIONS:
   The Scott Arboretum is in Swarthmore on Chester Road (Route 320) between I-95 and Baltimore Pike. Parking for the Scott Arboretum is just inside the entrance on College Road, on the left.

SKUNK HOLLOW

THE PARK:
Radnor Township, meaning "red district," was settled by Welsh Quakers who sailed to America on the *Lyon* in 1682. The Skunk Hollow trails developed by the township have been cut through the woods connecting Saw Mill Park and The Willows. No dogs are allowed in either of these park so don't continue past the terminals of these trails.

WALKS:
The Saw Mill (yellow) and Skunk Hollow (white) Trails flank the Little Darby Creek. The Skunk Hollow Trail is a linear walk and Saw Mill is an eye-hook trail. Both are heavily wooded. As of this writing, the bridge across the creek was out but you can walk the rocks across.

TRAIL TIME?
More than an hour.

TRAIL TERRAIN?
There are some sporty climbs in Skunk Hollow, especially along the Skunk Hollow Trail.

TRAIL SURFACE?
The dirt trails are well maintained but contain a dispiriting number of root knobs, tiny tree stumps and exposed rocks.

Ever consider what they must think of us? I mean, here we come back from the grocery store with the most amazing haul - chicken, pork, half a cow...They must think we're the greatest hunters on earth!

-Anne Tyler

> **BONUS**
> Although you can just about reach the nearby residences with a long leash, you can descend into this wooded hollow and instantly achieve a sense of seclusion.

TRAIL SENSE?

The trails are generously blazed with large swaths - so much paint was used, in fact, that the yellow paint seemed to run out as the blazes disappear on the Saw Mill Trail when it reaches the Little Darby Creek. The trailheads are marked with signs indicating hiking trails.

SWIMMING?

Little Darby Creek is a pretty stream but not deep enough for swimming.

ADMISSION FEE:

None.

PARK HOURS:

Dawn to dusk.

DIRECTIONS:

Skunk Hollow is in Radnor Township. From the intersection of Routes 3 and 252, take Route 252 North. Make the third right after crossing Goshen Road onto Saw Mill Road. Continue on Saw Mill Road to a small gravel parking lot at Saw Mill Park, just past the intersection with Earles Road. The trailhead is across the street.

If you pick up a starving dog and make him prosperous, he will not bite you. This is the principal difference between a dog and a man.

-Mark Twain

SMEDLEY PARK

THE PARK:
The personality of Smedley Park was transformed by the intrusion of the Blue Route. Smedley Park, named for the founder of Delaware County Park & Recreation Board Member, Samuel L. Smedley, features 120 acres of recreation squeezed against the rushing traffic of I-476.

WALKS:
There are two main trails in the park, blazed in red and yellow. The yellow trail is the stretch of the Springfield Trail which runs through Smedley Park. The red trail loops to the other side of the Blue Route.

You can also use the Smedley-Leiper Trail, opened in 1992. Frequented by runners, cyclists and rollerbladers, the paved path runs two miles to Leiper Park, former home of Thomas Leiper. Leiper operated an extensive milling and stone quarrying business on over 700 acres along Crum Creek. His Federal Period summer house, built in 1785, and four outbuildings overlook the park.

> **BONUS**
> SEPTA Trolley Line Route 101 bisects Smedley Park and the sight of the occasional car rumbling past is a glimpse at early 20th-century transportation. SEPTA maintains a fleet of 224 trolley cars, including a score of vintage models, which unfortunately are not regularly scheduled for Route 101.

TRAIL TIME?
   More than an hour.

TRAIL TERRAIN?
   This is a hilly location although none of the climbs is particularly harsh; only the trail along the Crum Creek through the picnic areas is flat.

TRAIL SURFACE?
   The surface is crushed gravel in the recreation areas of the park and rocky on the trails. This hard surface encourages the breaking of bottles at many places along the trail which threaten your pet's paws. The 6-foot wide Smedley-Leiper Trail is paved.

TRAIL SENSE?
   A park map is available to provide an overview of the property and the trails are well-marked.

SWIMMING?
   The Crum Creek is normally not deep enough for more than energetic canine splashing.

ADMISSION FEE:
   None.

PARK HOURS:
   Sunrise - sunset, year-round.

DIRECTIONS:
   Smedley Park is located between Media and Springfield. From I-476 (Blue Route) take Exit 2 (Baltimore Pike). Turn toward Swarthmore. Take the first left onto Paper Mill Road to the park entrance road on the left.

SPRINGFIELD TRAIL

THE PARK:
The creation of trails in most parks seems fairly obvious - use established animal paths or fire roads. But the Springfield Trail, linking four parks in a 5-mile loop roughly corralled by Woodland Avenue, the Blue Route and the SEPTA Trolley line, required vision and imagination of Springfield Township and private property owners in 1969 to bring into existence.

WALKS:
There are no shortcuts on the Springfield Trail; once you set off you sign on for the whole five miles. The strongest segment is from Jane Lownes Park to Smedley Park as the trail hugs the Crum Creek, often from a scenic ridge 100 feet above the water. Although it's noisy due to the adjacent Blue Route (the trail twice brings you directly beneath the superstructure) this is the walk to take if you decide to do an out-and-back. The hike along the trolley line from Smedley to Thompson Park is a wild and wooly excursion that brings you across train tracks, through dry creek beds, past ferns and wild roses and more. The quietest stretch on the Springfield Trail is the narrow trail along Whiskey Run. There is also sidewalking along Woodland Road to complete the loop.

TRAIL TIME?
More than one hour.

TRAIL TERRAIN?
This is a healthy workout. None of the climbs will bring you to your knees but they keep coming with dogged regularity.

TRAIL SURFACE?
The trails through the woods are dirt but you can encounter most any surface on this loop.

SWIMMING?
There are streams everywhere along the Springfield Trail but seldom is the water even a foot deep.

> **BONUS**
> The January birthstone: garnets. Mined for thousands of years, the ancients were said to have used the stone as bullets for the glowing red color was thought to increase the ferocity of the wound. Legend holds that garnets were carried by travellers to light up the night and protect from nightmares. Noah used a garnet lantern to navigate the Ark at night. Garnets come in every color and can even change hue in different light. And garnets were once mined along Crum Creek here so keep your eyes open on this walk.

TRAIL SENSE?

The yellow-blazed trail is well-marked through the woods but can use some touching up in the civilized areas around the trolley tracks and the roads. There is no map so you are dependent on these painted rectangles. The Springfield Trail, more so than most, is plagued by trail-obliterating fallen trees; even some of the blazed trees have collapsed into the creek. For navigation purposes, this loop is best executed clockwise rather than counterclockwise.

ADMISSION FEE:

None.

PARK HOURS:

Dawn to dusk.

DIRECTIONS:

There are no signs for the Springfield Trail, nothing to indicate it exists save for those yellow blazes. The easiest access is at Jane Lownes Park and Smedley Park. The entrance for Smedley Park is on Baltimore Pike, just east of Exit 2 of the Blue Route. Park in the Paper Mill Road across the trolley tracks and pick up the Trail at the Comfort Station. Lownes Park is off Route 320 with street parking along Kennerly Road.

TAYLOR ARBORETUM

THE PARK:
The ownership of this property dates to William Penn who sold a thousand-acre land grant to John Sharpless in 1682. Sharpless descendents operated grist and cotton mills here for nearly two centuries. Taylor Memorial Arboretum was established in 1931 by a Chester lawyer, Joshua C. Taylor, in the memory of his wife, Anne Rulon Gray.

WALKS:
The many trails through these 30 acres along Ridley Creek are short, interconnecting segments about evenly divided between woods and meadow. There are many highlights here, including plant-covered rock outcroppings, a bald cypress pond, and a groundwater spring.

TRAIL TIME?
Less than an hour.

TRAIL TERRAIN?
There is some slope on the property down to the floodplain of the Ridley Creek but the walking is easy.

TRAIL SURFACE?
Dirt and grass and pine straw.

TRAIL SENSE?
The trails are not blazed but a detailed site map is available. There is also a map board at the parking lot.

SWIMMING?
The water behind the Sharpless Dam in the West Woods is excellent for canine swimming. In the East Woods the Ridley Creek offers a small stone beach and fast-flowing shallows for a doggie whirlpool.

BONUS
The Taylor Memorial Arboretum provides a 12-Tree Self-Guided Tour. The collection is especially strong in Far Eastern specimens and spotlights three Pennsylvania State Champion trees: the Needle Juniper, the Lacebark Elm and the Giant Dogwood. Also on the tour is a Dawn Redwood, an ancient tree known only through fossils until 1941 when a botany student tracked down living specimens in rural China. Some of the first seed to come to America resulted in this tree.

ADMISSION FEE:
None.

PARK HOURS:
Daily from 9:00 a.m. to 4:00 p.m.; closed on major holidays.

DIRECTIONS:
Taylor Memorial Arboretum is located north of Chester. From I-95 take Exit 6 and follow Route 320 North. Just past 22nd Street, make a left on Chestnut Parkway and continue to Arboretum entrance, making a left on Ridley Drive.

TYLER ARBORETUM

THE PARK:
    Thomas Minshall signed a "lease and purchase" deal with his fellow Quaker, William Penn, for this tract of land in 1681. It remained in the same family until 1944 when Laura Tyler bequeathed the property to the public for an aboretum. This living tree museum was started in 1825 when brothers Jacob and Minshall Painter began systematic planting of more than 1,000 varieties of trees and shrubs, more than 20 of which still survive, including several state champions. The park today encompasses 650 acres.

WALKS:
    There are seven main trails that ramble up and down wooded hills, along ridges and through fields. All are wide and easy to follow.

    The white-blazed Wilderness Trail covers ten miles and requires the better part of four hours to complete. A better way to explore the Arboretum is to fill up the day with the six shorter trails. The Dogwood Trail in early spring is a must with the brilliant white flowers from the edge-growing trees in backdrop against the green canvas of the woods. The Pinetum Trail is a sunny walk through many of the special trees on display and the Painter Brothers Trail is the more dramatic of the two mid-length hikes.

    Tyler Arboretum is adjacent to Ridley Creek State Park and twelve more miles of hiking trails for the intrepid explorer.

TRAIL TIME?
    More than an hour.

TRAIL TERRAIN?
    Hilly in the woods, flat on the grassland trails.

TRAIL SURFACE?
    Natural dirt.

> **BONUS**
> There are many beautiful formal gardens in the Delaware Valley which of course you cannot experience with your dog. At Tyler Arboretum you can study trees (including a Giant Sequoia planted between 1856 and 1860), enjoy rhodedendron and azaleas and have your dog alongside.

TRAIL SENSE?
   The trails, all blazed, loop back to the Arboretum Center and are named. You can easily follow them without a map.

SWIMMING?
   Rocky Run and Dismal Run flow through the park but are more conducive to splashing than swimming.

ADMISSION FEE:
   $3.00 for non-members.

PARK HOURS/PHONE:
   8 a.m. - sunset, year-round. (610.566.5431)

DIRECTIONS:
   Take Route 1 North making a left onto Ridley Creek Road past Route 452. Turn left onto Painter Road and continue to Tyler Arboretum on the right.

We are alone, absolutely alone on this chance planet; and, amid all the forms of life that surround us, not one, excepting the dog, has made an alliance with us.
                              -Maurice Maeterlinck

UPLAND PARK

THE PARK:
> The Swedish settlers built a tobacco plantation in this area in 1644. They named it Upland; to the Lenni Lenape it was Mecoponacka. This urban park was once owned by the Salvation Army and used as a day camp for underprivileged youngsters for summer vacations. It was purchased by Delaware County in 1968 and today the park covers 60 acres.

WALKS:
> The park trail runs from the main parking lot down to the Chester River. It is narrow, trash-strewn and wooded. A decent walk can be parsed together by skirting the perimeter of the park along the treeline.

TRAIL TIME?
> Less than an hour.

TRAIL TERRAIN?
> The trail down to the creek is fairly steep.

TRAIL SURFACE?
> Dirt along the trail; informal trails are grass.

TRAIL SENSE?
> The trail is utterly unmarked and there is nothing to indicate there is any trail.

SWIMMING?
> There is no easy access to the Chester Creek.

ADMISSION FEE:
> None.

PARK HOURS:
> Sunrise - sunset, year-round.

> **BONUS**
> The focal point of the former Camp Upland is the redesigned and refurbished Redwood Community Theater. Over a hundred popular music and show performances a year take place here.

DIRECTIONS:
Upland Park is located in Upland. From I-95 take Exit 6 and follow Route 352 North. Make a left on Upland Avenue to 6th Street. Make a right to the park entrance on the left.

As a young lawyer, 19th century Senator George Graham Vest of Missouri, addressed the jury on behalf of his client, suing a neighbor who had killed his dog. Vest's speech has come to be known as "Tribute to the Dog."

The best friend a man has in the world may turn against him and become his enemy. His son or daughter that he has reared with loving care may prove ungrateful. Those who are nearest and dearest to us, those whom we trust with our happiness and our good name may become traitors to their faith. The money that a man has, he may lose. It flies away from him, perhaps when he needs it most. A man's reputation may be sacrificed in a moment of ill-considered action. The people who are prone to fall on their knees to do us honor when success is with us may be the first to throw the stone of malice when failure settles its cloud upon our heads.

The one absolutely unselfish friend that man can have in this selfish world, the one that never deserts him, the one that never proves ungrateful or treacherous is his dog. A man's dog stands by him in prosperity and in poverty, in health and in sickness. He will sleep on the cold ground, where the wintry winds blow and the snow drives fiercely, if only he may be near his master's side. He will kiss the hand that has no food to offer; he will lick the wounds and sores that come in an encounter with the roughness of the world. He guards the sleep of his pauper master as if he were a prince. When all other friends desert, he remains. When riches take wings, and reputation falls to pieces, he is as constant in his love as the sun in its journey through the heavens.

If fortune drives the master forth an outcast in the world, friendless and homeless, the faithful dog asks no higher privilege than that of accompanying him, to guard him against danger, to fight against his enemies. And when the last scene of all comes, and death takes his master in its embrace and his body is laid away in the cold ground, no matter if all other friends pursue their way, there by the graveside will the noble dog be found, his head between his paws, his eyes sad, but open in alert watchfulness, faithful and true even in death.

WAWA PRESERVE

THE PARK:
   Seventy acres along the Route 1 corridor have been set aside for this preserve. The Wawa Preserve is managed by the Natural Lands Trust.

WALKS:
   The Rocky Run Trail runs through this land, connecting with the Tyler Arboretum to the east and the Darlington Trail to the west. All told, the linear Rocky Run Trail stretches 2 1/2 miles, with the parking lot at the center. The section to the west (on the parking lot side of Valley Road), which parallels the appropriately named "Rocky Run," is the more scenic with quiet woods and stunning stream vistas. The trail is wide and easy to walk.

TRAIL TIME:
   More than an hour.

TRAIL TERRAIN?
   Most of the trail is gently rolling but there are several steep slopes to negotiate.

TRAIL SURFACE?
   Dirt, often studded with rock.

TRAIL SENSE?
   White blazes mark the trail and a descriptive trail map is available from Middletown Township.

SWIMMING?
   Rocky Run carved this attractive valley on its course to the Chester Creek. It is wide but not deep.

ADMISSION FEE:
   None.

PARK HOURS:
   Sunrise - sunset, year-round.

BONUS

In July 1920, Babe Ruth took his big four-door touring sedan on a Yankee roadtrip from Philadelphia to Washington. It was a jolly trip on the way back for Ruth, his wife and three teammates, including stops for bootleg liquor. Singing and driving much too fast past midnight, Ruth failed to negotiate a turn on Route 1 near here and flipped his car. No one was hurt and all walked to a nearby farmhouse to spend the night. Ruth returned the next day with a mechanic to look at the tangled wreckage in the daylight. When he saw it, he said simply, "Sell it." The entourage made their way to Philadelphia, greeted by newspaper headlines screaming, "Ruth Reported Killed In Car Crash."

DIRECTIONS:

The trail is south of Media off of Route 1. Turn right on Valley Road at the Wawa Dairies across from the Franklin Mint. The parking lot is within a half-mile on the left.

WOODLAWN TRUSTEES PROPERTY

THE PARK:

From 1850 until 1910, feldspar, used in porcelain dishes and false teeth, was mined here in the Woodlawn Quarry. You can still see the remains of these spar pits, with their scatterings of mica and other minerals. In 1910, as his campaign to preserve the Brandywine Valley intensified, William Poole Bancroft bought hundreds of pristine acres in the lush floodplain and rolling woodlands where the Brandywine Creek makes three wide, gentle turns. Bancroft formed the Woodlawn Company to manage these lands, harboring some of the oldest trees in Delaware. Today, the property, which straddles the Pennsylvania-Delaware line, is open for recreational use to the public.

WALKS:

These informal trails can be combined to create any kind of day out with your dog. Athletic dogs will enjoy romping across the grassy hills above the Brandywine. Walking back and forth on the Fire Trail along the water provides an easy 45-minute walk.

The trails can be jumping off points for hikes of several hours duration. Following the white blazes of the Wilmington Trail Club along the Brandywine River you can cross Smith Bridge Road and follow the trail up to Chadds Ford. This involves a short walk, with little shoulder, on Creek Road and the trail is too rough and narrow to keep a dog leashed comfortably. In Pennsylvania there are loops around the fast-flowing Beaver Run and around farmland. The trail is hilly and requires some careful creek crossings but is very scenic. Finally you can cross Thompson's Bridge Road and walk into the Brandywine Creek State Park.

TRAIL TIME?

More than one hour.

> **BONUS**
> Breaking out of the woods at several points on the hilltops you are greeted with an unparalleled view of Granogue, one of the more spectacular of the American castles dotting the Brandywine Valley's chateau lands.

TRAIL TERRAIN?
   Moderate to difficult hills leading away from the river; the fire road is cut on rolling terrain; the only truly flat walk is the trail on the edge of the Brandywine Creek.

TRAIL SURFACE?
   Dirt and grass, with some sections covered in wood chips and others using the remains of old paved roads.

TRAIL SENSE?
   The trails are unmarked, no map is available but orienting yourself to the river and roads should prevent any confusion.

SWIMMING?
   The shallow Brandywine Creek is an excellent swimming river for dogs with many easy access points from the trail.

ADMISSION FEE:
   None.

PARK HOURS:
   8:00 a.m. - sunset, year-round.

DIRECTIONS:
   The main trails of the Woodlawn Trustees are bordered by the Brandywine Creek, Thompson's Bridge Road and Beaver Valley Road. There are no highway signs to direct you here and the parking lots are not marked. The main access parking lot is opposite Peters Rock along the Brandywine on Creek Road. Other gravel parking lots can be found on Ramsey Road, Beaver Valley Road and opposite Woodlawn Road on Thompson's Bridge Road (Route 92).

Nearby Parks

ANDORRA NATURAL AREA/ FAIRMOUNT PARK

Philadelphia County, Pennsylvania

THE PARK:

America's first public park began with 5 acres in 1812. Today, Fairmount Park is the largest contiguous landscaped municipal park in the world with nearly 9,000 acres. It is home to an estimated 2,500,000 trees.

The Andorra Natural Area, at the park's northern boundary with Montgomery County, evolved from a 19th century nursery. Ownership of the property dates to 1840 when Richard Wistar named it "Andorra" from a Moorish word meaning "hills covered with trees." One of those trees - a massive sycamore - grew right through an enclosed porch in the house of the chief plant propagator of the nursery. The weakening sycamore was cut down in 1981 but the Tree House survives as the Andorra Visitor Center.

WALKS:

The main trail at Andorra is a 20-station Nature hike. There are also a dozen other named trails that branch off this loop. The Forbidden Drive also begins its 7-mile journey along the Wissahickon Creek to the Schuylkill River here. The Forbidden Drive, so-named when it was closed to automobiles in the 1920s, can be shortened by several bridges across the Wissahickon. In addition, there are many blazed trails climbing out of the Wissahickon Gorge from the Forbidden Drive.

> **BONUS**
> In 1855, a hotel entrepreneur built a new inn on Rex Avenue. To draw attention to his hostelry he constructed an Indian from old barn boards and propped it up on top of a rock overlooking the Gorge. In 1902, when the Indian Rock Hotel was long gone but with the silhouette still there, artist Massey Rhind was commissioned to make a representation of a "Delaware Indian, looking west to where his people have gone." The kneeling warrior has gazed up the Wissahickon Gorge ever since. A switchback trail leads to the Indian Statue where you can get close enough to pat his knee. And take in a breathtaking view.

TRAIL TIME?
   More than an hour.

TRAIL TERRAIN?
   The Forbidden Drive is flat; although the climbs out of the forested Wissahickon Gorge are steep, the trails are relatively easy walking once the task is completed.

TRAIL SURFACE?
   The Forbidden Drive is compacted gravel; the woodland trails are dirt and rocks.

TRAIL SENSE?
   The paths are blazed and a map of Andorra is available.

SWIMMING?
   The swimming is excellent in the Wissahickon Creek.

ADMISSION FEE:
   None.

PARK HOURS/PHONE:
   5:00 a.m. - 1:00 a.m., year-round. (215-685-9285)

DIRECTIONS:
   Andorra is on Northwestern Avenue between Ridge Avenue and Germantown Avenue.

BRANDYWINE CREEK STATE PARK

New Castle County, Delaware

THE PARK:
Once a du Pont family dairy farm, this spectacular tract of land became a State Park in 1965. Delaware's first two nature preserves are here: Tulip Tree Woods, behind the park office with majestic trees over 200 years old, and Freshwater Marsh, at the edge of the Brandywine Creek. The stone walls that criss-cross the 850-acre park are the legacy of skilled Italian masons who crafted the barriers from locally quarried Brandywine granite, the original "Wilmington Blue Rocks."

WALKS:
There are 8 blazed trails on both sides of the Brandywine. All are short, all are woodsy and all are hilly. The star walk at Thompson's Bridge is the rugged Rocky Run Trail, winding around the closest thing to a mountain stream in Delaware. Also at Thompson's Bridge is a Multi-Use Trail that follows the Brandywine Creek for about two miles. You can walk the dog across the Brandywine at Thompson's Bridge via a short, unmarked trail at the end of the boardwalk through Hidden Pond that leads to the roadway.

TRAIL TIME?
More than an hour.

TRAIL TERRAIN?
If you can't reach out and touch the water of the Brandywine you are moving up or down a hill.

TRAIL SURFACE?
Dirt; the Multi-Use Trail is embedded with rocks.

TRAIL SENSE?
All the paths are blazed and there is an excellent color map available.

BONUS

In the winter of 1802 a rudderless French immigrant living in New Jersey named Eleuthere Irenee du Pont was invited to the Brandywine Valley to hunt game. It was not a successful trip. The damp weather fouled his gunpowder and his musket continually misfired. It was so bad du Pont decided to re-enter the industry he had turned his back on in France as a youth: black powder. When it came time to launch his new business he remembered what you see today at Brandywine Creek State Park: the hardwood forests that would burn to charcoal, one of the ingredients he would need for powder; the abundant granite in the hills to build his mills; and the swift-flowing river to power the mills. And so he returned to Delaware to launch an empire. Incidentally, the favorite breed of dog for the du Pont family when they lived here: the greyhound.

SWIMMING?

The Brandywine Creek is one of the best places in Delaware to take your dog for a swim.

ADMISSION FEE:

Charged daily from Memorial Day-Labor Day and weekends in May, September and October.

PARK HOURS/PHONE:

8:00 a.m. - sunset, year-round. (302.577.3534)

DIRECTIONS:

The main entrance is on Adams Dam Road, between Thompson's Bridge Road (Route 92) and Rockland Road. Another parking areas is at Thompson's Bridge Road.

Any man who does not like dogs and want them does not deserve to be in the White House.

-Calvin Coolidge

FAIR HILL NATURAL RESOURCES MANAGEMENT AREA

Cecil County, Maryland

THE PARK:
This is the Godzilla of area hiking. Traversing its 5,613 acres are over 75 miles of multi-use trails. Many go through rolling hayfields as befits its stature as a leading equine training center.

WALKS:
The trails through the fields are typically doubletrack (old dirt vehicle roads). Singletrack trails dominate in the forested areas. The Big Elk Creek surges through the property and is spanned by many trail bridges, including one of Maryland's five remaining covered bridges. The Big Elk Creek Covered Bridge was built in 1860 at a cost of $1,165. When it was reconstructed in 1992 after sustaining extensive damage from heavy trucks, the tab was $152,000. Fair Hill is also a good place to walk by house ruins.

> **BONUS**
> Flying concentric circles outward from Philadelphia, Hollywood location scouts for Oprah Winfrey's movie project, *Beloved*, spotted the Fair Hill terrain and selected it as the backdrop for the film's rural scenes. A ramshackle 19th-century tenant farm was constructed and much of the movie shot here. The producers decided to leave the movie set intact, to deteriorate naturally. You can wander among the fake buildings and even knock on the styrofoam stones.

TRAIL TIME?
   More than an hour.

TRAIL TERRAIN?
   The stiffest climbs are in the vicinity of the Big Elk Creek but most of the trails are like walking a steeplechase course.

TRAIL SURFACE?
   Mostly natural trails, usually dirt.

SWIMMING?
   The Big Elk Creek runs swift and shallow through the park - deep enough for trout but not for dogs.

ADMISSION FEE:
   $2 parking fee.

PARK HOURS:
   Sunrise - sunset, year-round.

DIRECTIONS:
   Fair Hill is just west of Newark. Take Route 273 across the Maryland-Delaware State line until the first four-way intersection, Appleton Road, about 1.2 miles. There is parking down either side of Appleton Road. The park office is on Route 273, behind the grandstands for the Fair Hill Race Track.

FRENCH CREEK STATE PARK

Chester/Berks Counties

THE PARK:
A wilderness fort once stood on the small stream flowing through these woods which was garrisoned by the French during the French and Indian War and thus "French Creek." The hillsides here were dotted with charcoal hearths throughout the 1800s, fueling the nascent American iron industry. French Creek State Park was originally developed by the federal government during the Depression as a National Park Service Demonstration Area. In 1946, the area was transferred to the Commonwealth of Pennsylvania.

WALKS:
Approximately 40 miles of trails visit every corner of French Creek's 7,339 acres. There are 8 featured hikes of between one and four hours' duration. The marquee walk is the Boone Trail, a six-mile loop connecting all the major attractions of the park. All the walks are heavily forested with hardwoods - keep an eye out for the ruins of the area's charcoal-burning past.

TRAIL TIME?
More than an hour.

TRAIL TERRAIN?
There are many steep sections as you ramble about these wooded hills.

TRAIL SURFACE?
Dirt with frequent rocky stretches, especially on the slopes. Some trails make use of fire roads.

TRAIL SENSE?
All the trails sport distinct colored blazes. A trail map is available and you would be well advised to take it as the trailheads and junctions are not named.

BONUS
Considered by some as the "Orienteering Capital of North America," French Creek has developed a permanent self-guided course for the practioners of the art of map and compass. You can even challenge your dog's nose in a wayfinding contest.

SWIMMING?
There is abundant access to two lakes, the 21-acre cold water Scotts Run Lake and the 63-acre Hopewell Lake.

ADMISSION FEE:
None.

PARK HOURS/PHONE:
8:00 a.m. - sunset, year-round. (610.582.9680)

DIRECTIONS:
French Creek State Park is located north of Elverson. From Route 23 take Route 345 North to south entrance of the park on the left. From the Pennsylvania Turnpike the park is 7 miles northeast of the Morgantown Interchange (Exit 22).

OAKBOURNE PARK

Chester County, Pennsylvania

THE PARK:
John Hulme built the first granite shelter on this land, selecting the highest area on the property for his homesite. In 1882 a wealthy Philadelphia lawyer named James Smith purchased 143 acres of land on the west side of South Concord Road, including Hulme's house. Smith renamed it "Oakbourne" and set more than 150 skilled craftsmen to work refurbishing his new summer home. Oakbourne was soon the centerpiece of a 27-acre park with fountains, miniature lakes and rustic bridges. Oakbourne even had its own private railroad station and post office.

Oakbourne was willed out of the Smith family to the Philadelphia Protestant Episcopal City Mission in 1896 for the operation of a convalescent home for women over 21 years of age. The next 70 years saw thousands of female "guests" treated here before its costly operation overwhelmed its directors. Westtown Township saved Oakbourne from developers in 1974, eventually creating a 90-acre park.

WALKS:
Three connecting trails (Creek, Nature and Park) form a loop of nearly three miles to visit all areas of the park on both sides of Concord Road. The trails are all wooded, including native specimens and the remains of the Smiths' exotic plantings around the mansion.

TRAIL TIME:
More than an hour.

TRAIL TERRAIN?
There are some dips and rolls in some of the wooded areas, including one good climb on the Creek Trail.

TRAIL SURFACE?
Dirt and grass, with stretches of sand and rocks underfoot.

> **BONUS**
> The most striking feature of the estate was a 1,000-gallon, twin-tank water tower built on the lawn away from the mansion. Built of stone and brick to resemble a fortress, the tower features dormer-style twin roofs. James Smith installed the finest of telescopes at Oakbourne that offered views across the countryside of Chester and Philadelphia.

TRAIL SENSE?

The trails are haphazardly marked in places (the blazes are the smallest in Chester County) and can be hard to follow, especially picking the trail up across Concord Road. A map board is available between the parking lot and the mansion.

SWIMMING?

Part of the trail hopscotches past Chester Creek but, while scenic, it offers little opportunity for swimming, save for one deep hole under the railroad bridge. One of Smith's miniature lakes, encircled by reeds, is a pleasant canine swimming stop.

ADMISSION FEE:

None.

PARK HOURS:

Sunrise - sunset, year-round.

DIRECTIONS:

Oakbourne Park is in Westtown Township. Coming south on Route 202, make a left on Matlack Street, which runs into Oakbourne Road and South Concord Road. Make a right into the driveway and proceed past the mansion to the parking lot. Coming north on Route 202, make a right on Route 926 (Street Road) and a left on Concord Road. The park is on the left.

Dog. A kind of additional or subsidiary Deity designed to catch the overflow and surplus of the world's worship.
                                                    -Ambrose Bierce

RIVERBEND ENVIRONMENTAL EDUCATION CENTER

Montgomery County, Pennsylvania

THE PARK:

The Riverbend story begins 300,000,000 years ago when a crack in the rock known as the Rosemont Fault turned what would become known as the Schuylkill River a full 90 degrees. The first settlers came to the area in the 1500s when the Lenni-Lenape Indians began planting vegetables in an area known as 'Indian Fields." In 1904, Howard Wood, brother of steel magnate Alan Wood, created a 52-acre farm inside the river's elbow. Three generations later, in 1974, his descendents decreeded half of the farm to serve as a wildlife refuge known as Riverbend Environmental Education Center.

WALKS:

The feature trail at Riverbend, amidst two miles of hiking, is the Aloha Trail which circles the perimeter of the property. Unfortunately the walk is marred by the relentless pounding of traffic on the Schuylkill Expressway below. Look for Fiveleaf Akebia, an invasive plant which covers everything on the hillside above the roadway. The other trails are short connecting spurs of only several minutes duration. Avoid the Jack-in-the-Pulpit and Poplar Trails, which are overgrown. Also available is Sid Thayer's Trail, a linear trail on private property which is also plagued by traffic noise.

TRAIL TIME:

More than an hour if you hike the Sid Thayer's Trail.

TRAIL TERRAIN?

Riverbend is situated on the knob of a hill and there is little flat walking to be had here.

TRAIL SURFACE?

Dirt and grass.

> **BONUS**
> The Visitor Center is a restoration of a 1923 Sears & Roebuck mail order barn. A century ago Sears sold anything and everything by mail - including kits for building houses and barns. The kit, which could cost as little as a few hundred dollars depending on style, would include rough lumber, framing timbers, plank flooring, shingles, hardware, sash and paint. Usually shipped by train from the west, the barn kit would be loaded onto a freight wagon upon arrival and hauled to the building site for assembly by local carpenters.

TRAIL SENSE?
  There is a hand-painted mapboard at the parking lot for orientation. On the trails there are signposts at junctions. The Aloha Trail is blazed in red and marked by trail signs which are handy through the tricky residential passage.

SWIMMING?
  Riverbend sports the smallest pond in the tri-state area, alongside the Bluebird Trail. Although scarcely ten feet across, smaller dogs can motor around and larger ones can drop in to cool off.

ADMISSION FEE:
  None.

PARK HOURS/PHONE:
  Sunrise - sunset, year-round. (610.527.5234)

DIRECTIONS:
  Riverbend is in Lower Merion Township. From the Blue Route (I-476) North, take Exit 6A for Conshohocken, Route 23 East. Make a left on Spring Mill Road, continue past the Philadelphia Country Club and bear left at the end of the road to the Education Center parking lot.

VALLEY FORGE NATIONAL HISTORICAL PARK

Chester County, Pennsylvania

THE PARK:
The most famous name in the American Revolution comes to us from a small iron forge built along Valley Creek in the 1740s. No battles were fought here, but during the winter of 1777-78, when Valley Forge grew to be the third largest city in America, hundreds of soldiers died from sickness and disease.

America's attention was redirected to long-forgotten Valley Forge during a Centennial in 1878. Preservation efforts began with Washington's Headquarters and evolved into the National Historic Park.

WALKS:
There are four marked trails, plus miles of unmarked hikes. The Multi-Use Trail loops the Colonial defensive lines and Grand Parade Ground and visits George Washington's headquarters. Sweeping field vistas of the historic grounds are found all along the trail's six-mile length. The Valley Creek Trail is a flat, linear 1.2 mile walk along Valley Creek, past the Upper Forge site. Near the Valley Creek is the eastern terminus of the 133-mile Horse-Shoe Trail; the journey to the Appalachian Trail in Hershey begins at the Artificer's Shops on Route 23. Across the Schuylkill River is the 3-mile linear Schuylkill River Trail connecting the Pawling's Parking Area and the Betzwood Picnic Area.

TRAIL TIME?
More than an hour.

TRAIL TERRAIN?
The Multi-Use Trail is gently sloping across the rolling terrain; the Valley Creek and Schuylkill River Trails are flat, waterside walks. The Horse-Shoe Trail demands a steep and strenuous climb up Mount Misery, the natural southern defender of Washington's encampment.

> **BONUS**
> You can't find a more historical dog walk than this. The Multi-Use Trail rolls past reconstructed huts and parade grounds that transport you back to the Revolution. The National Memorial Arch, a massive stone tribute dedicated in 1917, stands out along the route. The inscription reads: "Naked and starving as they are, we cannot enough admire the incomparable patience and fidelity of the soldiery. Washington at Valley Forge, February 16, 1778."

TRAIL SURFACE?

The Multi-Use Trail is paved while the others are dirt trails.

TRAIL SENSE?

A National Park Service map provides locations for the trails and does not indicate the variety of side trails available, especially from the Schuylkill River Trail. Only the Horseshoe Trail is blazed.

SWIMMING?

Valley Creek is a delightful watering hole and the Schuylkill River is easily accessed for hard-core swimming canines.

ADMISSION FEE:

None.

PARK HOURS/PHONE:

Dawn to dusk. (610.783.1000)

DIRECTIONS:

The main park entrance is on Route 23 off Route 422. Parking for the Valley Creek Trail is on Route 252 (although the Foot Bridge is washed out as of this writing). To reach the Schuylkill River Trail, exit from Route 422 onto Trooper Road, make a left and continue back across Route 422 to the Betzwood Picnic Area or cross the Schuylkill River on Pawlings Road from Route 23 at the other end. Parking for trails here is on the right side across the bridge and also up the road at Walnut Hill.

WHITE CLAY CREEK PRESERVE/ WHITE CLAY CREEK STATE PARK

Chester/New Castle Counties

THE PARK:
William Penn bought most of this land in 1683 from Lenni Lenape Chief Kekelappen. Kekelappen was believed to have lived here in Opasiskunk, an "Indian Town" at the confluence of the middle and east branches of the White Clay Creek in the center of the Preserve. Of the many Lenni-Lenape Indian Towns in what is now Chester County, this was considered the most important. Frequent flooding over the past three centuries has obliterated all evidence of this former large settlement. In 1984 the DuPont Company donated the land which would become the 1,253-acre preserve. Many of the old structures from the early days of settlement are still visible. Another 2,300 acres adjoin the preserve in Delaware's White Clay Creek State Park.

WALKS:
The Penndel Trail, over three miles in length, is a superb linear trail which follows the east branch of the White Clay Creek, crosses the Middle Branch and continues along the main waterway into White Clay Creek State Park in Delaware. There are also eight miles of bridle trails across the fields and on the opposite side of the stream.

TRAIL TIME?
More than an hour.

TRAIL TERRAIN?
The walks are flat along the creek but there are plenty of hills elsewhere, especially if you continue into Delaware.

TRAIL SURFACE?
Dirt, with stretches of sand and rocks underfoot. The horse trails are often grass-covered. The trails are almost universally wide.

> **BONUS**
> In the southern part of the preserve is the Arc Corner Monument marking one end of the 12-mile arc which forms the Pennsylvania-Delaware state line, unique in American political boundary-making. The circular divide dates to William Penn's directive of August 28, 1701, when Delaware was still a part of Pennsylvania, known as the Lower Three Counties. A little more than 1/2 mile to the west is another monument marking the tri-state junction of Delaware, Pennsylvania and Maryland.

TRAIL SENSE?
The Penndel Trail (also the Mason-Dixon Trail in the preserve) is blazed in blue and a trail map is available.

SWIMMING?
There are many excellent swimming holes in the White Clay Creek.

ADMISSION FEE:
None. The White Clay Creek State Park in Delaware charges a daily fee from Memorial Day to Labor Day and weekends in May, September and October.

PARK HOURS/PHONE:
8:00 a.m. - sunset, year-round. (610.274-2900)

DIRECTIONS:
White Clay Creek Preserve is in southeastern Chester County. From Route 896 (New London Road) make a left on London Tract Road. The office is at the junction of London tract and Sharpless Roads. Parking Lot 1, further up London Tract Road, is the northern terminus for the Penndel Trail.

No one appreciates the very special genius of your conversation as a dog does.
              -Christopher Morley

www.ingramcontent.com/pod-product-compliance
Lightning Source LLC
Chambersburg PA
CBHW060721030426
42337CB00017B/2955